Shades of Suede

Cendaña Lova

Paperback ISBN: 979-8-9882207-1-8

Book Design by Our Galaxy Publishing

A collection of pieces inspired by healing, uprooting, hip-hop, and self-reflection. You see and feel every girl I've been in all stages of my womanhood — love, heartbreak, anger, empowerment, grief, celebration, etc. All happening at once.

Whether subtle or grand, every movement of life can change the shade of the suede. It looks different, its texture changes, it stains.

But it's because of this, that the suede belongs to you and only you. You call it your own.

Hoping to speak to anyone in need of light or shared struggle.

I give you my first literary baby. She's hood and spicy, but also soft and eloquent. Versatility.

One love,

C

for Maddie

Pulsing ticks, no idle hands on the clock

The story is not over…

shall we walk?

tunnel in 3am harlem
Harlem, NY
Short in stature, he marvels at her...
and wonders...
where does this *VOICE* come from?!

This freely-sounding melody
made of effortless hums
bouncing off of the walls of this
empty tunnel's drums

The soft vibrato is strangely startling
But calmly invokes an emotional smile of her guest,
starstruck and impressed

Her voice penetrates the grooves of the walls,
illustrating new markings
like graffiti'd bathroom stalls

soon to be buffered like public park protocol

Walls, walls, walls
all around me... Let yours down!
Sing... belt!

Fuck it,
be off tune!

Hit every riff
How can a body look so damn stiff
and still!   disguise pipes behind those lips!

Let yours down,
it's been so long and overdue

Never forget the angel song
that lives inside of you

my first sonnet in the mirror

Manhattan, NY

I told her, "Be patient," this is all new
She sees something in you, what's wrong with trust?
A reflection of time past is in you,
rays of light showing particles of dust

The image is dirty and imperfect
I blink to sharpen what looks back at me
Make a quiet promise to be fervent,
loving the painful layers tenderly

An exciting story comes from living,
celebration and grief can coexist
Hold sadness in the act of almsgiving,
stuck in inspiration and still find bliss

Pulsing ticks, no idle hands on the clock
The story is not over; shall we walk?

release
Panhandle, San Francisco, CA
Never thought that in order to find me,
I had to lose you

Never thought that a love so deep
could turn so cold
that even the frostbite doesn't numb me

You were the crime
We were the handcuffs
Our story was the prison

I have never felt freer

72nd street station
Manhattan, NY
Sometimes I take myself back in time
by turning the dial on my mind
rewinded to the times
when you were the only source of my rhymes

You used to be all I ever wrote about

Never finding inspiration in different places off route

I stayed and never strayed
but then the path started to fade
and the cement wouldn't stay
so I lost my way

But there was one thing I always knew

Our history was the compass...

so with relentless recollection
I replayed our memories for direction

Like psychosomatic reflection,
my body followed suit and looked back in objection...
like, *how are you lost?*

You know this path like the back of your hand
but I think life was tryna get me to understand

To turn a new leaf,
uniquely classified as my palms
cracked from neglect,
requiring eucalyptus balm

Symbolizing the parts of my life that I put on hold
fighting for our future and how I always expected it to
unfold
but I had to let go of that mold

It got rotten and old
and I had to remind myself
that there is so much more
to love and life
already written on God's scroll

I tell myself...
just move with patience

6 years later...
and I'm at 72nd street station

I don't think you've ever been here
but I live here,
now...

How I got here without you,
sometimes I still don't know how
but I promise...

I'm doin' well

And this new story I have to tell
doesn't have you in it

The soul's windows are the eyes
but I guess mine were always tinted

But like rings on an oak tree,
you can see how you have aged with me
in ways where you have stayed with me

No matter how much time goes on,
our memory lives on

There is stillness in motion

shroomies
Guerneville, CA
Equipped with floaties resembling tires,
we hiked to the river
Scorching hot sun,
immediately stunned
by the sting of ice cold shivers

Letting the river current take over
and sway us down south
We find one another
and link legs en route to its mouth

The *shushing* of the water
feels like bullies to our laughter
We listen and grow silent
and look up to the clouds

I awaken to my girl passing me a backwood
and look around at all of them
rotating floating backwards

Still connected,
we glide in the ripples of bliss
Enduring complete relaxation

… until it hits

With heavy eyelids
I open them up to the sky
and see it consumed with what looks like Sauron's eye
I tuck my head inside my hat
to erase my anxiety
The beginning of a suffering I experience quietly

The girl tattooed on my arm is coming to life
like she's trying to squirm herself out of my skin
Fallen trees have half sunken into the river
and their branches mimic a mystical dragon

In panic, I switch my gaze to the woods
an orange fox trods past
and hurriedly scurries off

Helpless and scared
I felt like death was taunting me
Every layer of mother nature
felt like skeletons haunting me

My surroundings would melt into kaleidoscopic skulls,
treacherous obstacles replaced the previous river lulls

Poisonous foods have tainted
what should be refreshing otherwise
A beautiful daydream,
now,
severely compromised

versa(still)ity
Lincoln Tunnel, NJ to NY
I think about where I come from and the people I left
Still doin' the same tired shit
Then "*still*" feels stagnant

Then I think about who I was back then
and who I am now
I'm *still* the same person
So "*still*" feels authentic

Still is breathing in the present
…being present…

Still is grounded stance like rooted plants

Still can feel blunt like ya stuck, high as fuck
Still is impatience…   like where the fuck are the changes?

Still is frozen when the world is in commotion
Still is a snapshot of water's erosion

Still water is *still*…   water
Waves are disturbed peace, but *still* fluidity

Tsunamis are *still* bodies…
of water unchanged
Properties remain nevertheless the same

Whether it's the ripples of the bottom
or the gravity of its fall…

Water masks distracting noise pollution
A treaty with concrete jungle, a peaceful resolution

dome secrets
Harlem, NY
My secrets revealed in echoes,
because I chose banter beneath the dome

Letting the hidden depths of me
spill out my oral cavity
I speak here in safety,
in confidence no one would repeat it

But as the words leave my lips,
it's my own voice I hear
betraying the covenant and whole purpose of coming here

Talk less, listen more

Silence is oftentimes our best teacher

TALK YO' SHIT

I cook up some courage on the stove you gaslit
Word on my lips, preach it like a chaplain

an homage to hip-hop
a lil' mix of Def Jam flavor and cypher juice

freestyle rap bars off the dome,
- intentionally unfinished and untouched -

dudes be in the doghouse
Manhattan, NY

                    spit on "Act Up" by City Girls beat

People ask me how I'm living and I keep it real
I tell em shit gets lonely but you know I deal
I'm used to being the cool chick keeping her lips
sealed
but trust, baby even when I'm sleep, my eyes are
peeled

I peep the shady shit you all pretend you don't do
All the shit on the low she think you won't do?
It's happening too much, I get up in my head
Questioning the skin I'm in, like ima have to shed

But I'm not built like you, that's what snakes do
You claim you keep it player, but you looking fake
smoov

Think it's simple like shedding skin makes you right
your wrongs
Give my flowers to you snakes, while I write my songs
Give my Garden of Eden to all you satan serpents
Preach my piece and drop the mic and I close up the
curtains

Never call you out or shout you out, it's not important
But the wrongs that sit inside me, man, I can't ignore it
I store it
I write it down
shit, maybe record it
Post disturbing content, all you viewers go report it

Now you lucky I'm not the type to expose you,
Don't wanna taint your image to people who know you
I'm sick n tired, y'all get off so fuckin' easy
Let me pull up my sleeves and have you sleazies hear
me

Barking game and think it's cute like a Sparks game,
but females run the court, you running like the narcs
came

It makes me hot you think you had a shot and not get
caught
Don't put the blame on me like I'm the reason bitches
fought

When I'm tried, I tend to hide what's on my mind
Not the type to pick a fight or make you choose sides
It's the disrespect that's eating up my insides

I'm nauseous, gagging like word vomit
Bouta spew out like a rocket,
out projectile, like I lobbed it
All the lies you tell your girl, ooo!
That bitch bought it
Me? ...I caught it
I know the game too well, it's like I taught it

You slippin' and slidin', watch the piso mojado
When you slide up in my shit, you lack pimp bravado

Got a dude I grew up with
Now expecting his own kid
with a girl I never met but I think I know

Should I tell her though?
That he told me he love me and I'm good for his soul?
I'm thinking, fuck no

That I'm the only chick
in his life who really tried to know the real him?
If I let him fuck, I'll prolly still steal him
but we was too close like family,
I could never feel him

Even saying that on the track make me feel phony
He couldn't have me so I guess he had to clone me
In his dreams he bones me
He even straight up told me,
that he see me in you
and you don't even know me

I heard you live with your girl, huh that's kinda cute
You turning 30 now,
I think it's time you do

I peeped your new boo
but to tell you the truth
I'm slightly confused

I can't tell if you her man, or if she got two
She real close to your friend,
Who is it, him or you?

Man I hate that dude
Surprised you don't do too
He got a slap on the wrist for sneak dissing you
You go on and call him brother
but I know your mother
She raised you better than that,
and I still love her

You shoot me a birthday text when she lay sleep
What you really wanna say is you stay missing me
I miss you too, fool
The only one I'll admit
I'm texting you, she next to you
sharing the same bed we did

I know you sleeping next to her but you feeling alone
Trust me, my boy
I know how that feeling go
How many years gon' pass us by before we fully let it
go
You give 99% to any bitch that come after me
That last 1 will forever be reserved for me

i be fuckin' around
Manhattan, NY
                 spit on "Sei Luv" by Messy Marv beat

Spittin' like a pimp
cause I be feeling worked up n shit
It's a lot a muthafuckas that be in my shit
Thinking shorty just a pretty face, but

Bitch, I'm it
I get articulate

Keep a dictionary in the back
like Iceberg Slim
I'm slim thicc' on em
I ain't no gangster pulling licks on none

Just a shorty from the stack
Steady laying on the mack
I got you so tight
Looking like you need more slack

Boy loosen up
Your ego looking to' up from ya shoes n up
Let me keep it a hunnit, so no confusing ya
If it's between me n you, man I'm choosin' up

You just a brother I got intimate with
Ima tell you what ya problem is
You think I'm sensitive
Acting comfortable like I ain't got this schedule fixed
Ain't no reschedulin'
Fake balla' like you drafted to the Pelicans

Love me a gentleman
Sticks and stones may break my bones
Might have to fake a moan
I wanna feel your stick break apart my skeleton

Time's a wastin'
No more time to talk
I move fast like the second hand on the clock
Staying at my crib like you got keys to the lock
Messy like a baby bib, make no sense when you talk

I need an intellect
I got a heart to protect
No cummin' inside unless you comin' correct

You thought you bagged me?
Last time I checked
You was third down the line
Nobody else to select

I got options, b
and y'all corny muthafuckas who be bullying me
Calling me names, asking me if I'm legally a midget
but these same muthafuckas out here asking me for
digits

Don't play with me!!
You ain't safe with me

I just don't give a fuck enough to chase no sleaze
I stack so much bread to make enough to freeze
I'ma chase my cheese
and say cheese for the camera
you see all my teeth

playa shit
North Park, San Diego, CA
Bitches got hoes too
I just don't talk about it
I used to lack courage
But now I finally found it

Bitches can be playas too
When I really wanna be
But I choose you like Donnell
You where I wanna be

Fuck anybody who like to
patronize and criticize
Clown at how I'm fun sized
But really fantasize
what's between my thighs
And all the ways you wanna tie
me up and fuck my brains out

My brains showin' out
So now I'm not only sexy as fuck
I'm an intellect with a dump truck
But I don't pack trash
I save lives to collect cash
I could strip too if I wanted to
And shake my fat ass
And watch your testes turn blue

Bitches not the only ones on their hands n knees
You not the only one holding Benzo keys

I don't need to wear grey sweats
to show off my package
I could wear the baggiest sweats
You still see what I'm packin'

Everything you want packed into a little mini
You can even "put me in your lil pocket"
I'll keep you fresh off the linty
'Cause your side piece dusty

bums n broke bitches / weezy f baby inspired
Manhattan, NY
How many licks til the center of a lollipop
How many licks do it take til the gun stops
They say brick when it's cold
You hit a rim shot
You salty like the crystals, my tequila rim shot

I juke left, juke right,
make you break ya ankles
You moving broke man,
You ain't got no bankrolls
You play too much,
the champion of Texas hold 'em
If you talkin' real loud, you lackin' real scrotum

I ain't no groupie hoe
I'm first class
You boarding Group E, hoe

Write you 26 letters,
like I covered the alphabet
Constant power trip between us,
we suffer when alphas bet

It's a useless wager,
You a ruthless player
No point in trying
to buffer the vampire slayer

You make up your own rules
Fixing shit with the wrong tools
Spinning out like yarn spools
Pickin' fights like lethal duels

I cook up some courage on the stove you gaslit
Word on my lips, preach it like a chaplain
Full of bone but fragile like a wounded shin
Pacing back and forth stupid like a glitched Sim

illmatic
Queens, NY
Word to Nas
He inspired this lil piece
In the projects where most times
they don't know or see peace

Constant street warfare and brothers on your neck
Robbing legacies of all the time they had left
Temporary tomb stones laid on the streets they wept
Shots to your back, taking lives like gangsta theft

Living in the projects
I feel comes a different sense of pride
A special way of life
There wasn't time to ask why

You had to get up 'n get to it
the moment you opened your eyes
And when you make it out alive,
the whole hood was surprised

slim shady slang / eminem inspired
Manhattan, NY
Double or nothin' I need me an Omar Epps
Cuffin' or fuckin, I need all the reps
Pepper in a flavor, spicy to your picky taste buds
Some o' you slip 'n sloppy like you sweat soap suds

Itchy cravings like a fiend
An uncomfortable scene
I slather hydrocortisone cream
from my neck down my inseam

Hives like bee houses
Currency like honey's money
Honey comb my nappy hair
Sometimes it make me look funny
Iron out the evil stares
of the demon in the mirror
screaming out your crippling fear

Light the Sage in early June
My best friend a Gemini
Her pupils diamond-shaped
I see gems in her eyes

Christmas lights outline the balcony
Noise pollution like street cacophony
A buffer to New York City
A rat to a stray kitty

Lavender in the diffuser
to calm the feelings that confuse her
the emotions that abuse her,
you loser, why didn't you choose her

Confidential trash,
need me a shredder to properly dispose

Left a gash on my back in senseless wrath,
now all your secrets I dare to disclose

Palms is too stiff
to curl 'em into fists
My wrists be too precious
so I fight with words like a lyricist

Project heat, I'm sweatin',
can't control the radiator
Fraudulent feet, you creepin',
you caught like a room raider

Binoculars from six floors up
I'm popular like Kith storefront

Garage parties with the hotties
Hennessy in my hot toddy
Surrounded by nobodies
Beautiful body like Gaudi taught me

Hit the marijuana before I sit at Benihana
Punctuate your run-ons, stupid,
make use of grammatical commas

Last of a dying breed
Foul necrotizing weeds
Poisoning the healthy soil
of loyal souls to the seed

Sewage stench in your raps,
can't handle the smell of decay
Make me listen to Mac Dre
and get the look on my face
like you know where I stay

free game fridays / la russell inspired
Bed-Stuy, Brooklyn, NY
Conversations with the homies feel like life lessons
When I talk, it's like I spit on open mic sessions
Wanna do it like Larussell
Talk my shit like a rehearsal
So you really hear me speak
and spit it right back in reversal

Rep the nickel n dime but didn't grow up on coin
Fuck a jugular, I hit ya femoral right in your groin

I tend to over complicate the bars that I spit
Simple blessings hold close like a car and a crib

It gets cold on the east around this time of the year
Icy world of isolation, bring a gangsta to tears

Stay up and be easy G, we all just tryna live
In a time of toxic riches, we forget life is a gift

Only borrowed for a time, we breathing out on a loan
My mama just a call away when I'm feeling alone

I got holes in my shoes where the soles should be
I got holes in my heart where my soul should be

Ya can't trip if you double knot the shoe lace
Leave my mark up on your bed, they my love stains
I run a soul train the way I penetrate your brains
I'm all you bitches' soulmates!
Hella people come to me, I'm a safe space
Unpack your trauma, baby, air out your suitcase

I learned to glamorize, romanticize the mundane
Case of the Mondays
That's what slackers say
What's the order of the week when you grind everyday

Weeks be feeling like a blur
Can't believe the dates
Write five pages,
start with a clean slate
Ump call me home safe,
Unc' wanna make a plate
Bump an Aaliyah tape
Wish she had on a cape
Smoke on the fire escape
Shift like tectonic plates
Shook til the jello shakes
California earthquakes
Call it my birthplace

haystack
Pill Hill, Oakland, CA
Sticker books and diaries
with doll-pocket sized keys
How I used to express myself
when I had sore knees

Juvenile arthritis
ain't gon' stop me from writing
Mama got the touch like Midas,
together we gon' keep fighting

Disney princesses and Barbie were never my idols
More like Kobe and Shaq when they won 3 titles

Raised a tomboy ever since I could remember
I remember even more when we get together

I feel like my father's third son
I never grew up with a sister
My mama was our queen,
and my brothers always kissed her

I grew up in a household that didn't know fists
but words and affection always ending with a kiss
My parents still strong and I'm learning everyday
the unfortunate reality that marriages rarely stay

I was taught by example
and my parents never lectured
They didn't have to break their back
to paint a perfect picture

They just keep their faith in God
and live their lives with his guidance
Prioritized their love
in the midst of all the fighting

They never let us see it
Either that, or they didn't feed it
Instead they filled our stomachs with
life lessons on how to lead it

Had my brothers playing instruments
and my parents harmonizing
How I got this music taste and lyricism ain't surprising
Although I never thought I'd spit to beats in advertisement
These pieces ain't for you
No part of me is compromising

RIP

Crown Heights, Brooklyn, NY
Take a seat it's honestly serious
I didn't know how to tell you
Express my feelings with this
But you gon' listen to this
For all these months I been pissed
And I ain't looking for forgiveness
Time reveals your fakest friends
I've come to terms with this
I'm not concerned with him
or your relationship

Shipwreck
I'm on your neck
Did you forget
Void on a blank check
Write me a check
For all the therapy sessions
To keep your phony ass in check

Sometimes I wonder what side of the story you sellin'
Or wonder what type of time you be on and you be
tellin'
Maybe you staying quiet but not 'cause you grown
But 'cause you know you fucked up
You ain't got a mind of your own

Flash a lil money and he cop you some nice
He hanging off your ear but he not talking nothing nice
We turning 15 years and now you cold as fuckin' ice
I known you half my life
And now you wanna be his wife?

I admired who you were
and you were always loyal
Now I'm pouring water over dead soil

Man I think it's kinda funny
How a grown ass man
out here asking me for money

I was homeless and jobless
Stripping my wallet
Thinking that my girl would always do me a solid
Like she always has
'cause that's what family do
But I guess family feuds
But over this dude?

He almost left you
For being friends with me
Ain't you see the problem, B?

Remember when we cried together 'cause shit was
getting hard?
How I illuminate your life when it feels so dark?

Well I hope your life is looking, feeling bright now
and that you happy playing house with "Mr. Right"
now
He gon show you soon enough that all he is, is Mr.
"Right Now"

And when he does,
don't hit my line cause that's over now
I got some toilet paper for all your salty tears now

Ain't give a fuck we fell out
You left me in the cold
You moving like a sell out
I see your soul is even sold
So to you, my best friend,
I really thought we'd grow old
We were locked in
But it's a wrap and I fold

But my point is, why is the gun loaded?

strap
Somewhere in the air from JFK to SFO
You leave me with nothing but stab wounds
from knives not meant for me,
from sharp blades of childhood,
from old wounds that keep getting picked

Never fully healing,
but oozing open with blood
at the sound of anything even remotely triggering

And see... who are we?
To tell people how to feel
about something we can't see

Something that lives inside of them... who are we?
To tell them
they cannot be triggered

But my point is...   why is the gun loaded?
Why is it always loaded...   and ready to be pulled?
Why do you pull the trigger...   at things I would never think to load it
for?
Why do you grab for it...   at things I would never cop a glock for?

The point is,
you shouldn't be strapped
You shouldn't have that thang on you
like you ready for murder

Cause it's a scary brother move
Moving like you ain't got shit to lose

You stepping heavy in those shoes
Carrying weight on your back to your own rhythm and blues

forever damaged
Manhattan, NY
I'm doin' penance
to attempt to cleanse your lenses
of wrongful vengeance

You harbor punitive projection
Perpetually sickening perspective
You will never see the goodness in females
as a collective

It's not my fault you choose to
disclose your past
like stripping clothes of your back

Cause when you start,
you don't stop
You gotta take accountability
for the wounds you inflict on innocence
because of the permanence
of your life's plot

At a certain point, baby, you gotta heal
You grip your trauma so tight
like you're scared ima steal
the emotions it made you feel...

Like I'll excise it from your body,
You've mistaken it for a vital organ

It's a tumor, sweet love
removing it will make you born again

paradox
Manhattan, NY
Hating you is killing me
It's so hard to be mad,
it sucks the soul right out of me

Hating you is painting the canvas black,
when there were so many colorful memories on our palette

Hating you is closing my eyes to the sex scenes
Blinding myself to the good parts of our movie,
Cause sex all night doesn't make the fight right

Hating you is forgetting I hurt you too

Hating you requires energy
reserved for loving me

Hating you is burying my feet in wet sand
for temporary strength and permanence,
but even the sturdiest
of sand castles still get washed away

Hating you is regret,
and I don't regret you

Hating you is something I pretend to do

Hating you is pointless
because, still, through it all,
I listlessly love you

dirty love
Bushwick, Brooklyn, NY
You drag my soul through dirt,
expecting me to play in it

Sprinkle dirt on my face,
to camouflage me so I stay in it

My face stained black no matter what I try do
traces of what you left and your traumatic residue

I clean my face hard
to exfoliate the black tar
seeping deep into my pores
hoping it doesn't leave scars

Like wind, you disrupt order
Questionable stability,
perhaps more fragility

I dig deep in my dirt
to stencil the placement of my new roots
So the next rush of disturbances
won't knock me off of my boots

27th birthday self-incarceration
Ukiah, CA

(prequel to *release*)

For 4 years I did time
I wrote you letters I never sent
I cried for you in my cell
I fantasized what life would be like with you when I got out
I made goals of how I was gonna make up lost time

People would visit me
like clockwork
Do their visitation rounds
Just to peep if I'm doin' well
Tell me they missed me
but I knew it wasn't shit

Why didn't *you* visit me?
Those visiting hours were for you,
why didn't *you* tell me you missed me
I can't even remember the last time you kissed me
I self-convicted myself
I didn't have to stay here

So I decided to post my own bail
release myself from a prison I put myself in

4 years spent defining my life on account of you
Doing time on various counts of you

When I told you this was *my* day
the one day that's about *me...*
It makes sense that I stand up for myself
on the one fuckin' day
that it's about me

the ugly sonnet
Manhattan, NY
My body has stripes from constant slashes
Struck with insults you don't mean and take back
I'm sick of drying salt off my lashes
You are dirty clothes on the discount rack

My striped skin is worth more than charity
Disguising me as homeless and broken
Your mouth contaminates my clarity
Beyond grandiosity unspoken

I bear the weight of this embarrassment
to deem you lovable beyond measure
My heart is fragile, it knows where it's been,
but you play with it for selfish pleasure

An unrecognizable reflection
Your wounds melanate a scarred complexion

Discover Stevie Wonders
in your eyes
while feeling blind

the pretty sonnet
Manhattan, NY
My body has not known laughter like ours
Enraptured with my cerebral capture
of your smile, that sends me straight to the stars
Time stands still, I will it to go faster

Your hands know hard labor, calloused with skill
I call them home to interlock with mine
Quiet your mind, I hear it working still
Lay your head on me, under the moon shine

My voice is your favorite song; I will sing
lullabies until I enter your dreams
You deserve restful slumber, my sweet King
Scared to wake you up, the way my heart beams

I will hold you 'til the sun wakes the birds
I love you without saying it in words

foundation
San Leandro, CA
I've heard that, bricks were so old they could write novels

Can you imagine the novels our houses could write?

Mold starts to grow
White paint fades to cream
Floor boards creak
Bones get weak
The smell of home changes to aged wood

So as we grow up in these houses and make them our homes…
they, too, are growing…   aging…

I start to reminisce on the times I never thought were gonna end
Childhood, to put it simply

But a memory does not expire
if your memory does not retire

Keep them close to you
Talk about them so they never stale

Pass them on to your kids
Or better yet…
Pass them on to your parents

Tell them every single memory,   inside joke,
conversations you had with your siblings
'cause they spend their whole lives trying to be the best parents for you

I wonder if they ever really know

They planted the seed and let it grow…
          so,
show your parents the seed that grew

The flowers you all blossomed into…
          because of the water they poured on you

My parents are my home

While I age, they age too…   I forget that

Let us strengthen our bones

Let us take care of our homes

mama's mama

San Leandro, CA

I know my angels are still with me
I feel them everyday
More when I'm sad,
comforting my loneliness in the only ways they can

I never knew you, Mama,
so why do I feel your energy so strong?

There are things I know in my heart that I feel like you've taught me
I truly think I loved you and held you in a past lifetime

I wish I knew you
I wish I could call you and even know what you sound like
I wish you could sing to me
I wish you could cuddle me as tears well up in my eyes as I write this

I feel you so close to me
and I hate that I've never had you close to me

If I ever get to meet you or marvel at how gorgeous I imagine you were,
I would love to tell you stories…
of who I am
so you know me too

You didn't even know your daughter as a woman
But she's lovely, Mama
She looks like you
and I, her   …so I belong to you, isn't that beautiful?

Please know that your legacy has carried on through storytelling

You sounded absolutely pure
and although I can't touch you,
I indulge in every embrace I have with
every piece of you, you've left on this earth

My mother, my aunties, my bloodline

So I wonder…
Do you have to be known first to be forgotten?

the bells
Manhattan, NY

(inspired by "The Bells" by The Originals)

The thing about music is
it takes you back to a time and place,
to someone's face,
and every time I hear this song

I see you with my eyes closed
My heart knows…
It could never forget how it goes

We were just kids,
raising each other,
talking bout our kids
See, we were friends first
so the love transcended beyond limits

And I hear about you from time to time
but you're not on my mind…   not as much
Truthfully, I…   lose touch the more we're out of touch

Not sure who you are or what you like anymore
but I love that young boy…
          to my core

And as beautiful as we were,
what makes us painfully sweet
is that we will always be connected

Every part of me

and when every layer of me listens,
I can still hear them ringing
as if it's you singing

Long live the bells
Long live this story we tell

I wish you well

casual talk
Manhattan, NY
Things ain't gotta be so deep
for me to peep
what you giving off
Is it cool if I keep
my gaze on you?

I feel like living soft
and just having casual banter
sprinkle some seeds in your mind's planter
be the reason for your heart's lantern

you know, somn' light

Cause lookin' at you feels warm
like a campfire in the forest
You got me feeling elevated,
and no blunt even sparked this...
                    casual conversation,

We ain't even gotta flirt
I just wanna see you be yourself and shed off all these
nerves

No pressure, love
You don't know what you're teaching me
By just exuding authenticity,
you give off...
                    sincerity

And I feel like that's the part that's missing

It's a lot of folks just walking round here... existing
            talking without listening
                        cocky and self-christening...

but I'm just tryna talk to you

Discover Stevie Wonders in your eyes, while feeling
blind
Have your voice compose the melody
and your words carry the cadence

Your presence is overwhelming,
but I love inhaling your fragrance

You know what I'm sayin' like,
deprive myself of senses but still... find you

In a field of flowers,
my favorite scent is you...

     I think God sent you

and I don't even like flowers all that much
but you put a dozen you's in a floral bunch
and I'll wake up and smell the roses
just so I never lose touch

Complement your day without compliments
Shower you with attention to release any tension
I'm selective with how I dispense my coin
but if it's time with you I gotta spend...
I put that on my dime 'til the end

My hands react to fake love
It turns my fingers green
So I tell the lady at the store that I need more rings
I wanna build and foster trust
I mean... you know, among other things
but understand it can't be lust
You know real bling don't rust

So I'm meticulous with its care
I wanna cradle your past
I know I'll never be your first,
but can I be the very last...   girl that you kiss
before I give you a daughter?

I wanna raise her in a home to see a love that never
falters
and truthfully,
it don't matter to me,
if we ever meet at the altar

Just love me in front of her so real love is all that
haunts her

acid trip
Milpitas, CA
"Cry...
Just cry..."

Eliminating the need
for performative scenes
who other than you three
to be completely free

"Cry...
You just cry..."

It felt like four hearts beating in unison
Compensating to keep the energy polarized
Like a wolf pack, we protect and run deep
I need my sisters more than I realize

Glued like we shared wombs,
we gathered on our girl's bed
An affinity so attuned
electric waves connecting our heads

I rest my head on one's shoulder,
the other resting hers on my thigh
the third rubbing my back
as I just...
cry...

I just have to cry...

No words were said
No sounds but the rhythm of my woes
with theirs to follow, a community prose
Shared among the girls I love best
I can finally rest

coach pops
Hayward, CA

another sonnet

Just the right amount of tough and gentle;
couple pushes and shoves while he taunts him
Physical contact strengthened our mental,
fell to the ground as the ball touched the rim

Time froze and we all rushed to his rescue
I remember the quick change in color
to dark purple as the swelling came through,
this perfect sunny day is now duller

My tough guy rises in heroic stance
frustrated, but smiling to show bravery
Limped off the court with his victory dance,
escorted him to the car, carefully

A man strong enough to break down boulders
My father today, a wounded soldier

Is it that I'm abandoned or constantly running?

tracks of my tears

Clinton Hill, Brooklyn, NY
The amount of tears these tracks have seen
I could look Smokey Robinson in the eye
Squinting 'cause I got smoke in my i-ris(k)
my life getting on the train this late in the night

What is it...
about getting on transit
that makes it painful to sit
through the journey

As if the slides of life passing through the windows
signify my journey

I guess this means I'm a city girl

Interrupting my thoughts,
I watch the girl
              across from me
stare out on the platforms as they pass by

Her eyes pulsating left and right like nystagmus
Wondering if she, too, is in mental life analysis

The speed of the train
makes subway life look like film negatives unraveling
Imitating time traveling,
I'm forced to refrain
from falling off of the rope I'm straddling
between true contentment and pain

Too fast and blurry
in too much of a hurry

There is no conception or perception of
what I see in the reflection

Too dismissive and weighed down
by the darkness of my plight

But if I just take a second
and put the negatives up to the light,
I'll see the whole picture

Even still, I sit here aimless
while the train conductor remains nameless
The tears I weep leave me shameless
to the strangers I came onto this train with

just hurts less
Manhattan, NY
My pen is losing its ink
and I didn't even know it was running out

So many unfinished sentences…
            incomplete thoughts…
words half written
            interrupted
almost as if the thought never existed

Tear drops are punctuating my sentences
before they were done
Falling sporadically as they please,
blurring the faded ink of my written pleas,
confusing future me
when she rereads this…
what old me was even trying to convey

What was I even trying to say?

Do I go in and retrace the missed strokes?
Do I leave it blank…
Do I keep space for the unknown?

How often do I sit in sadness,
knowing it's mandatory for transformation

How many nights have I had in private
- that even if I tried to explain it out loud -
will never amount to how severely tough
each night really is

How it feels too regular
like laying out my uniform the night before school
knowing the dress code never changes

How it doesn't get better…   just hurts less

How I don't get stronger…   just numb to it

How the cries aren't cathartic…   I'm just exhausted

From pulling myself out of heartache I put myself in

Reaching for my own hand in hardening cement before
it is married permanently into streets,
the ones I drive late at night
just to clear my mind

I don't want to become jaded of pain...
like I'm used to it
tired of making room for it
moving like I can zoom through it,
Through the cracks
like it's new highway construction
on the self-made destruction I've created

We can't leave cracks in the ground and
keep teaching ourselves how to jump

Ruining our stride
like pressing the gas over the speed bumps

I'm tired of these hurdles,
I just wanna walk

Tired of feeling on edge
like I'm swimming with sharks

Maybe my pen is losing its ink
'cause I'm losing my spark

Maybe the words aren't making the page
cause my story needs to change

Maybe even my own book is tired
Subliminally boycotting tradition
Begging me to start talkin' bout some else
Like when you puttin' out the second edition?

Maybe the gaps are a favor to me -
intentionally allowing me to forget the thought
so I stop...   writing about it

Maybe they're the reason this feeling doesn't make sense anymore

Maybe that's a good thing

i'm tired
Ka'anapali, Maui, HI
When is it my turn?
All this patience
all this reflection
all this clarity I search for...
all this time I spend in solitude
all this bullshit...

for what?

Who am I even asking?
Who am I even talking to...

It seems like lately,
I forget what my voice even sounds like

When is someone gonna answer me?
When is it my turn?

God, show yourself to me
Please...
I'm losing faith

I don't know how to save myself anymore

I don't know what makes me happy anymore

In exhausting search of something I don't even think exists anymore...

Is it that I'm abandoned
or that I'm constantly running?

What if what I'm yearning for doesn't even bring me happiness
like I think it will?

What if I'm always going to imagine life with someone I consciously
chose to leave?

What if I'm the one who abandons everyone else?

And this loneliness, this quietness,
this grief,
is my karma for abandonment

even this, I spend alone
Wailea, Maui, HI
Part of me wants to call you and cuss you out
as if it'll be some sort of
release...   revenge...   or finality

But you've hurt so many people,
that my hesitation to do so
comes from knowing that my scars
will never be deep enough to matter to you

Merely blemishes you can soften with apologies
or so you think

When you're a veteran at hurting people you love,
does each person's pain even affect you anymore?

Do you care that,
to me, my scars have reached bone...
or does that not matter to you
because other women have died from theirs?

Do the holes in my heart you've burned through
- that I now bleed thru -
mean anything to you?

Or is that just one more thing I have to experience alone?

heavy is the head that wears the crown
Manhattan, NY
All the things about me that I'm proud of
are sometimes…
the same things I'm tired of

I love that my presence is like
        oxygen to your collapsed lungs
but,
tired of being inhaled only when you are suffocating

I'm proud that I left home,
        and everything that I know
but,
tired of starting over

Happy that I overcame fear
of traveling independently,
let my feet touch ethnic soil on
all hemispheres,
but,
sad to turn to my left and see that you weren't here

Love that my soul is one of a kind,
years beyond its time
but,
so over being the right girl, wrong time

Consciously choosing to continue to heal
but,
annoyed that I'm the only one doing it;
with no one to build anything close to real
feeling nothing but foolishness

Proud to be irreplaceable to you
but,
tired of being the girl held responsible
for you never moving on

Tired of being the girl you still love but choose not to have
The one you still dream of,
so you choose to stay awake to fight thoughts of me

Tired of being the girl people reflect on but,

never blessed to be genuinely genuflected upon

I wanna be proposed to, too

Impressed that I continue to break free
and fly with clipped wings
but,
so over being the girl that got away

It's not that sweet

Confident that the love I want
will be rooted in friendship
but,
fear that friendship is all it will ever be

I'm just tired of being the one they wish they could do
over
Tired of being the girl people appreciate later

Why do I get all the trial runs
all the guinea pigs,
all the test dummies

All for them to learn from the best
just to put other girls above me

I'm honestly just fuckin' tired of being resilient

Tired of being self-sufficient

Proud of being admired from a distance,
but
only as someone they used to know

Not someone with whom they want to foster growth

I remember the girl you used to know

I abandoned her, intentionally
when I lured into seduction of a version
I couldn't fathom of her, previously

A better one

The grown one

The one I am now
who foolishly contemplates,
debates her strengths
cupping them at arms length
like she is weighing them on a scale

The exhaustion is inevitably heavier,
tipping her unbalanced
manipulating herself into thinking her talents
are wrongfully debilitating

At peace,
knowing I was every single one of my exes' best friend,

but
all to still be alone in the end

what was *you* doin' in 2020?
San Francisco, CA
I remember protesting in the streets of Frisco
when George Floyd couldn't breathe
Seeing a sign held by a black nurse that said,
"What color am I when I'm saving your life?"

~ ~ ~

You see in the year 2020 I had corresponding vision

2020 vision, I saw too much death perfectly
2020 vision, that fuckin' year saw the worst of me

Struggling to un-see
the constant catastrophes
obliterating the masses
hoping each time I'm seeing the last of these

Isn't it crazy
that the only room I can step inside...   feels like suicide

                    Bedside...

forced to put the fear and anxiety aside

This is a place I know.

A place I belong,
a place I've studied

I've had a patient describe me like a piece of dynamite...
Small, but mighty

And as we're sharing laughs at the bedside
I'm just hoping he don't die tonight

                    Bedside...

"Nurses are the real heroes"
... yeah, aight.

                         Tell me, how can I save you
                         when I feel everything BUT pride?

I feel lost,
scared, like a kid who gotta gear up for war
in a suit that don't fit me

Strap on boots that fit feet twice as big as me

I feel oddly,
responsible

Like who the fuck else but us?

Our own doctors ain't steppin' foot in the room
Trigger happy behind computers
flicking the joysticks
controlling us like minions

Watching us dressed and decked in
hazmats
like I'm sprinting face first
into a cloud of laughing gas

This shit ain't funny

The media's now calling us frontline workers

And the rest of ya'll lucky to be sideline lurkers

Bitch, we been here!

Ain't no fuckin' 9-5...

we LIVE here

They gave you work from home privileges
And some a you were still outside acting frivolous
Spreading the virus
without giving a fuck about the rest of us

So I guess I also feel anger

Daily announcements in huddle...

"Reuse the same mask all shift"

You ever think maybe my face is the mask?
The one I put on every shift?

The good and smart nurse
excited for work
bejeweled with germs
dazzling my navy scrubs
to be an employee of worth

Tell me again, how can I save you
when I feel everything...

                    but pride, right?

          That's what I should feel?

I'm not ungrateful,
I'm just...   confused

How did we get here?

I don't want to make things worse
and make it about me
but no part of any part of the reality in this,

is actually about me

The death count looks like penny slot spins
The hospitals were never short on body bags before

We don't even say their names

But thank you for the flowers,
I'll put them on my patients' graves

change the narrative
Manhattan, NY
Expecting different credits
after watching the same film

Wanting summer after winter,
when I know spring comes first

Soon you will exhaust from repeating history

Crying the same tears,
lethargically following a devastating manuscript
you already know the ending to

harsh sun
Manhattan, NY
Get the fuck up out of bed

Do you feel me kissing you?
Do you feel the blanket of love
I'm covering you with?
I get up everyday so *your* body
knows it's time for you to do so, too

Work with me
Look up at me
I'm waiting for you to smile back
Open your swollen eyes and meet mine

Look,
I brought you birds
I brought you foliage
I brought you breeze

I brought you movement in the streets
proof of life,
Wake up and relish your gift of sight

Good morning, my love
Everything glows in light,
It's time to get up

last words
Soho, NY

(the yin to *RIP's* yang)

Today, I developed an old roll of film
Nervous, because I can't remember what's on it
Dropping it off to the woman towering over the glass case

Hesitant... gripping the camera,
tapping my index finger on the lens,
anxiously asking it to awaken
and remind me of its contents

Nostalgic, like leaving keys on the counter
of the empty apartments I've moved out of

Hearing my thoughts echo against the vacated space
That was once filled with life lived

Reminiscing on moments that have never happened
Frankly, the moment just felt...   sad

Shaking my head at the thought
of reliving another story that has already ended

...at how much I'm leaving on the counter

A feeling similar to leaving my heart on the doorstep
in subtle hopes you'll open the door
and trip over it

Just to remind you that I'm still here...
            that I'm still beating
                        that I'm still alive
Still figuring it out

Still holding my head high,
when you were the one who crowned it
in times when all I saw was the ground, it
mattered to me if you ever found it

Did you ever care to look around for it?
or,
did you step over it on the way to get in the car of your
man
to take you so far away from me...   from us

Hypnotizing you into a fairytale land
I didn't want to let go of your hand

I wish I knew when we'd get high and watch Friends
I wish I knew when we shared the same bed
that those sleepovers would eventually end
So I wouldn't have to deal with this broken heart I now
have to mend

We went through everything together

It's like we didn't want to grow up
And now I'm grown up
and you're all glowed up
from the happiness I always longed for you to have

I see the smile on your face I never thought I'd see
But somehow I always predicted its beauty
'cause when *your* heart beamed,
mine smiled back

When *your* heart bled thru broken skin,
mine toughened and thickened
in protection of you;
coagulated to guard the gates from flooding
out of wounds...

My perspective of you
was identical to the one of mine
You see, I saw me in you

So I guess when I look at your smile,
that you have because of him and the life you have
now...

It makes me emotional

No, not because I'm not around to witness it
But because it's prettier than I imagined it would've been
I knew happiness was inside of you
Oh God, how I prayed it would spill out of you
I wrote you words that I painted and framed
Words you put up into wall art
The ones I stared at when I laid sick in your bed when
I first moved here

Alone
I wish you could see how much I've grown

You don't even know where I live

My best laughs were with you
over jokes dating back to childhood
when boroughs didn't separate us
and we lived in the same neighborhood

That's how deep we run
so I'm confused how you didn't know
that you could've just sat me down, girl

Woman to woman
And told me what it was

I would've respected you more

And what's crazy is I already know
that your therapist
is telling you, you deserve this

Knowing you,
you're easily skewed

You just eat up simple concepts
Beautified with fancy forceps
Start to live your life,
thinking you cut out the nonsense

But I never thought I was the nonsense

We were a sisterhood I still can't put into words, and
I'm a poet now, remember?

So I apologize if I'm rambling, but...

I guess the shades of suede don't change the same on leather

If we are constantly evolving...
will we ever be finished?

God's prayer
Manhattan, NY
How come the silence is so loud when
the lights are off?
I'm in my bed...   naked
                    with all my clothes off

The silence is deafening,
it's like it's tryna silence somn' else
My racing thoughts inside my head
like it's someone talking other than myself

Tossing and turning, I can't sleep
so I turn on my back and I breathe deep
Sigh in and out slowly, I know I can't count sheep

You are the company that you keep
though,
so I talk to God

Life got in the way,
and I'm ashamed to say that I forgot

Some people never see God unless they get shot...

Hey God

Gimme a sign everything's gonna be okay

That my body,
        my heart,
                and my mind
will always be safe...   here where I lay

I pray the sign is divine;
whether its obvious or,
hiding behind, whether
its love in constant rhyme or,
love in a partner's mind,

I pray...
the sign you send me is all mine

Another year I get to continue narrating my story
Smile at my past and present,
and marinate in all its glory

The silence is growing peaceful
now I can hear the rain
drip-dropping on my window pane
so I,

        release my pain

Fall into a slumber,
        lost count of the number...

counting sheep never worked for me anyway

Thank you God, in your name, I pray

big girl
Manhattan, NY
I know I'm growing up
'cause my problems don't feel like the end of the world

My happiness is my shiniest pearl
and my everyday stride is my prettiest twirl

I loved and I lost
and I gained both times

I learned to train my mind
to make music with wind chimes
when otherwise,
the storm would shake my life

I used to cry like every part of me was breaking
but now I see lessons in the reflections I'm making

It's like I changed my perspective
I'm more receptive
to things outside my control that used to feel deceptive

sweet solitude
Manhattan, NY
                        (sequel to *tunnel in 3am harlem*)
I clear my throat
because I value the delivery of my speech

With conviction, I plant my feet
declaring this sterile field breached

And as I do this, I notice...
the straggler leaves
graze the concrete, tickled by the breeze

Softly caressing the tunnel to awaken...   whispering...

        She is here again
        Alone this time

Park gates of steel whistle ghostly
as the wind blows through them

Traces of whips in the distant night,   riding blade on curb
Not a witness in sight,   I am so undisturbed!

I BASK in this solitude

My self-chosen aloneness

It is here in this moment
that I matter the most

Engulfed in peace,
allowing the gust to sweep
me away in its current

I am born to flourish

In a library of variable factors
and a book of fluctuating chapters...
        the constant Word is You

You know what you came here to do

allow yourself
Manhattan, NY
How lucky are we that we get to grow up?
Age does not scare me
I don't fear the discovery
of the older woman I'm becoming and will become

I no longer have any expectation
or final destination
of what the woman I look or feel like should be
- at the end of my healing -

What does *"fully healed"* even mean?

If we are constantly evolving...
            will we ever be finished?

If we know that life is to be lived, not conquered...
            why do we question if we will win it?

If there is no perfect person...
            why is the goal to completely fix our flaws?

Wouldn't that just lead us to loss?

If nothing is ever promised,
why do we walk, hooking pinkies with life...
            timid and shy,
            knowing interlocking hands is more secure?

I'm sure...
that being a student of love
has taught me so much more
than independence has

Sometimes independence feels like...
a toddler timeout
facing the wall 'til I stop crying
                        ...'til I've had enough
                            ...'til I fall asleep,

from tired grimaces or,
near misses or,
life expectations unrealistically listed

Independence feels like,
we have to put the time in...
for allowing infiltration
like letting ourselves love is the deadliest sin

but how beautiful of a life have I had because of it?

How many different loves have I had because of
fearlessness?

How empowering is it
that the reason I have known pain and heartbreak
is because at some point...

I allowed it

I allowed my vulnerability to take control

I don't want to know who I'd be without it

I don't have it all right and figured out
but I lose sight
that THIS is what the healing's all about

So the next time you feel like you have to be fully
healed
in order to let yourself love again...

Remember this -

You peel back different layers of yourself
each time you fall in love

You are ever changing
always lovable
everlasting
and forever discoverable

So I hope you never close your heart

Love is its own musical
and how blessed are we
to play our part

'93 til
Manhattan, NY

the year we all turn 30

Empty advice
Constant reminders to not compare

You're not hearing me...

the thing is, I don't care

I don't sit here and wish my life was theirs

or that my life was still...

over there

I'm saying, I'm approaching an age
where I'm supposed to have shit figured out

I ain't put a lot of pressure on life plans n shit

but shit,
not even a man to KINDA grow with?

Not even a partner to stay up all night
seein' if this shit is even worth it?

Not even a second to take a breath
at how my eggs
may not even be its healthiest?

Not even a backyard to grow a garden
my children will pick fruit from
the way they are my own seeds
blossomed from my bosom...

Not even any of that?

Wait, is that society's expectation or mine?

What the fuck do I even have in my name...

Fuck that,

what I have IS my name

This name means something

These poems... mean something

This life I've made... MEANS something

They mean everything

I gotta change my perspective
and get it in my head
that if God wanted me to have all those things at 30...

I wouldn't have any of the things I have now at 29

I have me

    I have integrity

        I have grace

            I have patience

        I have my pen

    I have value

I have you

Acknowledgements

To my parents - You are the reason I grew up loving art in every form. I hope this book shows you that I take you both with me everywhere I go.

To my brothers - You both are my lifelong best friends. It's the three of us 'til the grave.

To my sisterhood and childhood friends - Thank you for being a part of the journey you now see in words. You've had to listen to me while it all happened, so in some ways, y'all lived through it with me. You know who you are.

To the men, whom some of these letters are addressed to - simply, thank you.

To my mentor, Lani - Thank you for seeing me and believing in me. For sharing this world with me in a way that has birthed my own voice.

To everyone near and far, who I might touch - I hope to meet you one day. Thank you for your time, and placing value on my words. I hope you feel seen.

about the author

Born and raised in Hayward, CA, Cendaña Lova is a Filipina-American, who started writing spoken word poetry in high school. She realized her love and passion for it in college and throughout her 20s. Her professional career as a cardiac nurse has taken her to San Diego and now New York, where she can also be seen performing at open mics in Manhattan and Brooklyn.

Just another shorty from the Bay, growing into her 30s - she is the perfect balance between a nature-loving, sun girl and an insatiable, metropolitan hustler. Where West Coast meets East, she brings that Bay Area flavor to New York crowds every time she gets behind the mic. Shades of Suede is her first chapbook.

Kobe forever.

cendana.mad@gmail.com